TO... _____

DREAMING OF A SCOUSE CHRISTMAS

TWAS the night before Xmas and all through the house
Spread the beautiful pong of me old Lady's Scouse.
The stockings were hung on the black leaded grate
For old Daddy Xmas and Rudolph his mate.
Me mam in the pinny and me in me wellies
Were eagerly waiting to fill up our bellies.
We polished the stair rods and dust off the mat,
Loaded the sideboard with this and with that.
Two crates of Threllies and a few dozen brown,
For friends and relations who are coming to town.
A bottle of port and some white Aussie wine,
Some bunloaf, some bis and a trifle so fine,
A bottle of rum, me Dad's special stock,
A ham and some whisky he got off the dock.
Our presents were wrapped and hidden away,
We knew where they were but we just wouldn't say.
New boots, new socks and a red woollen Jersey,
We'd be togged out like toffs, the pride of the Mersey.
The old girl said, "Now lads be off to your beds",
With a wipe of our noses and a punch on our heads.
So me with the poes, our kid with the candle,
We'd trot up the 'dances' it was too much to handle.
We'd lie there awake and cover our heads,
As the rest of the family all went to their beds.
The lights from the farmers drew squares on the ceiling,

We couldn't get rid of the wide-awake feeling.
Then, like magic, I suddenly woke.
The long night was gone and our kid gave a poke.
"Gerrup, La" he whispered, "You know what I mean,
"Sneak down the kitchen and see if he's been."
I heard someone down there, the fire was on.
I peeped around the corner, yes he'd been and he'd gone.
Me mam was so busy with the meat in the oven,
Our kid came behind me, pushin' and shovin',
For this magic morning we'd waited all year
And now it had come: "Cor La, it's the gear!"
Our toys were all scattered all over the mat,
Lead soldiers, a train set and a fire-Bobby's hat.
The box that they hid on the back kitchen shelf,
Was a neat model Spitfire you build by yourself.
Our stockings were special, far better than any,
An apple, an orange, a bright shiny penny.
I realise now that me Mam, bless her soul,
Had brought us all up with me Dad on the dole.
Christmas ain't tinsel, puddin and trees,
But parents with shiny-faced kids on their knees.
It's kids strutting round in their shiny new shoes,
Not turkey, wrapping and bottles of booze.
Remember those years, don't it strike you as funny,
We had barrels of goodies without any money.

Author Unknown

"*It's* beginning to look a lot like *Christmas*"

"Happy, happy Christmas, that can win us back to the delusions of our childish days, that can recall to the old man the pleasures of his youth, that can transport the sailor and the traveller, thousands of miles away, back to his own fireside and quiet home!"
Charles Dickens
The Pickwick Papers

Above: Taking root – Christmas arrives in Church Street as workmen set up the seasonal gift from the council to the city in 1952
Right: Kelly's Eye for a bargain. Plenty of time to wrap up well in time for the Christmas of 1967

Above: Crosby meets Crosby – Bing Crosby was singing about a White Christmas while over in Little Crosby in 1981, the snow is falling crisp and even

Above: The most talked about grotto in Liverpool – Blackler's – where a young Beatle George Harrison once worked as a trainee electrician. The giant Santa remains a golden memory for so many children who reluctantly turned into adults

Above: Capital of Christmas – Liverpool's Bold Street was once deemed our very own 'Bond Street', the equivalent of London's elegant shopping thoroughfare. In 1972 Bold Street was beautifully illuminated

Opposite page: Forget Blackpool's golden mile illuminations, Church Street in 1975 was an equally electrifying experience
Right: Fowl play was welcome at ER Hughes in 1967 with a turkey a real steal at 10 bob, what a poultry sum

Top: "No luv, it's not a Liver Bird." Good humoured haggling over a turkey at market in 1967
Bottom: The traditional Christmas Tree Bashing tournament opens on Formby Sandhills in 1992. No one loses – everyone gets to take home a tree to celebrate the season in Sefton

*"Christmas is a time for giving,
A time for love, for fun and living"*

WE ARE NOW PACKING
PARCEL "D"
CONTAINING
4 LBS **BEEF** BONELESS
½ LB **TEA**
½ LB **BUTTER**
2 LBS **CHRISTMAS CAKE**
1 LB **BACON**
1 LB **SAUSAGES**
1 PACKET **SWEETS**
6 **ORANGES**
1. Nº **2** JAR **JAM**

Above: The glorious Goodfellow charity in operation packing parcels at Cooper's Store in 1934
Opposite Top: It looks like the January sales but, hold on, this is December.
Last minute shoppers get in a festive frenzy in 1963
Opposite Bottom: Post Office staff at Victoria Street sort the Christmas mail in 1966.
Your card is probably still there — you should get it next week

"Walking in a Winter Wonderland"

Above: Ice dreams are made of this. David and Christine Salisbury of New Brighton walking in a Wirral Wonderland – Eller Park in Wallasey

13

Festive Flashback – Sefton Park, January 1959

"Oh, don't fall – it's
slippery,
"Be careful, it's icy in
Sefton Park."
"Cor, mum . . . dad, it
looks just like a huge
Christmas card,
"All these statues covered

from head to toe . . . in
snow"
The lake was frozen: trees
were shivering and ducks
were all alone,
I warmed to the promise
of hot chocolate at home.
"Can we come tomorrow?"

I said, giggling behind
silver-topped trees.
"Oh please . . . my
snowman's nearly done."
Mum and dad smiled,
"C'mon now, we will –
but be careful son."

Top Left: When I grow up I'm going to be a farmer and then I'm going
to let all the turkeys free. Oh, I'm going to be late for school now, I'll
ask Santa for a Mini Cooper tractor next year – the 1968 version
Top Right: Skate expectations: Strictly come dancing for fun at
Calderstones Park in 1966
Bottom: Deer friends – Alan and Claire Bolger feed Thumper in 1979

"*Flakes fall from the sky like the fluff from a torn pillow*"
Extract from a schoolchild's essay, St Hugh's Primary

"ALL I WANT FOR CHRISTMAS IS YOU"

"Sing hey! Sing hey!
For Christmas Day,
Twine Mistletoe
and holly, For a
friendship glows,
In Winter snows,
And so lets
all be jolly!"

Above: The infamous Grotto Girl Gang at work. "You keep him talking while I tug his beard and run off with the prezzies." Sharon Donoghue and Pauline Williams have a Santa Summit in 1968
Right: Location Location Location. Hazel Wolfe plans a conservatory extension while checking out this Clayton Square des res doll's house in 1955

Above: Festive fun in Fazakerly, 1956. Round and round the Merry Christmas tree, orphans from Liverpool Cottage Homes blissfully dance.

Above: A celestial chandelier lights up busy Church Street in 1963

Right: Relatively speaking – some ghosts of Christmas presents for all the family as Lewis's announce their own war against a miserly credit crunch in 1989

Opposite top: Toy Story – 1980. An Aladdin's cave of colour in Lewis's famous gift emporium.

Opposite bottom: Baubles, fairy lights and tinsel – the delightful decorations department at Lewis's

Christmas Gifts for all the Family

INTEREST FREE CREDIT
12-month, interest free credit on all Furniture and Floor Coverings over £200.

LEWIS'S NEWSFLASH
For a purchase of £75 or more in any of the following departments, a period of 6 months free credit applies.
Major Electrical Appliances, Audio, Televisions, Bicycles, Light Fittings and Accessories, Power Tools, Fire Surrounds and Heating, Small Electrical Appliances, all Household Textiles and Curtaining, China, Glass and Cutlery, Continental Quilts over £99.

Please ask for written details.

MONTHLY OPTION
OPEN A ACCOUNT AND YOU CAN DO A MONTHS SHOPPING WITH JUST ONE EASY PAYMENT. APR 30.6 MAY BE VARIED. PLEASE ASK FOR WRITTEN DETAILS.

GLASS & CHINA GIFTS
THE GLASS AND CHINA DEPARTMENT IS FULL OF EXITING GIFT IDEAS FOR CHRISTMAS, THOMAS, PORTMEIRION, DARTINGTON, DENBY, WEBB, WEDGEWOOD, POOLE, ROYAL WORCESTER, ARE JUST SOME OF THE FAMOUS NAMES IN GLASS AND CHINA THAT ARE AVAILABLE IN OUR BASEMENT.
FROM THOMAS WEBB Crystal Chatsworth Whisky Tumbler Only **£2.75**
FROM WEDGEWOOD a great Christmas Gift Idea, Child's Christmas Plate, 1980, Second in a series for young collectors. Only **£7.95**
FROM DARTINGTON a Victoria Candle Holder Only **£9.25**

T.V. GAMES
ATARI VIDEO COMPUTER SYSTEM Complete with 27 game Combat Cartridge **£99.95**
Wide range of cartridges available including Space Invaders at **£29.95**
FROM OUR EXTENSIVE RANGE OF GRANDSTAND ELECTRONIC GAMES INVADER FROM SPACE the Game of Cosmic Combat **£19.95**

LEWIS'S RECORD DEPARTMENT HAS ALL THE LATEST LP'S AND SINGLES AT DOWN TO EARTH PRICES.

BLONDIE "Auto American" L.P. or Cassette **£3.99**
BARRY MANILOW "Barry" L.P. or Cassette **£4.49**
DR. HOOK "Greatest Hits" L.P. or Cassette **£4.49**

And there is a wide selection of LP's and Cassettes to suit all musical tastes.

Fashion GIFTS
COSY PYRRENEAN Ladies Dressing Gowns—Button thru and wrap over styles from **£39.99**
NYLON WAIST SLIPS, side split from waist to hem **£4.99**
£3.99
Matching Camisole **£2.99**
and matching French Knicker
FANTASTIC RANGE of Tootal Ties, plain or fancy designs from **£1.99**
MATCHING SCARF and Tie Sets in pure wool **£6.99**
THE PERFECT CHRISTMAS GIFT—A personalised T Shirt or Sweat-shirt. Prices from **£1.95**
Hundreds of Transfers to choose from at 50p and 95p and we will put your name on free!

TOY FAIR
VISIT OUR FABULOUS

CUSTOM, DELSEY, SAMSONITE are just some of the famous names in our extensive

TOP CHRISTMAS GIFTS IN 1955

For Mum:	Scarves
Gloves	Handkerchiefs
Handkerchiefs	Slippers
Perfume	Cigarette lighter
Cosmetics	
Table Napkins	For John:
Stockings	A magnetic
Undies	football game
Knitwear	Card games
Slippers	Mechanical toys
Stationery	Annuals
	Ball pen
For Dad:	
Gloves	For Jane:
Socks	Dolls
Ties	Woolly toys
Cigarettes	Handbags
Pipes	Gramophone
Books	records

"Dreaming of a Blue Christmas"

Above: Everton fans queue up for a Goodison goody – the hope of bagging a
ticket for an FA Cup tie against Sheffield Wednesday in 1947
Opposite Top: "Please Santa can somebody buy me a week's holiday in Majorca
to see out 1982 in style and sun!"
Opposite Below: Super Santa's back in town for his annual Blackler's Grotto
stint in 1986. He had to do it, there was a Claus in his contract

WINGS HOLIDAYS TURN BRASS MONKEYS INTO BRONZE GODS.

...avel agent or ring 01-2... ...200 now.

"ROCKING AROUND THE CHRISTMAS TREE"

"Everyone's dancing merrily in a new old fashioned way"

Left: Three stars – Tommy Steele, a frequent visitor to Liverpool stages as Scrooge, points out another star in the night sky to Speke starlet Claire Ryan

Right: Poptastic performer Tommy Quickly, a Merseybeat legend, makes waves during a Christmas visit in 1964

23

Above: Oh Carols! No, not Neil Sedaka, but a rocking, rolling 'beat' service at Liverpool Cathedral in 1964

Above: And a Salvation Army played . . . Clayton Square is alive
to brass and tambourines as Lord Mayor Alderman Livermore
switches on the lights to the sound of seasonal music in 1958
Right: Wherefore art thou? Disco daftness comes to Romeo's
and Juliet's where extra mistletoe is brought in during 1977.
Wings may have been Number One that year with *Mull of
Kintyre* but Abba were chasing with *Name of the Game*

Top: "Right, it's all mapped out," said Fred Talbot the
Weatherman, wearing last year's Christmas pullover:
"It's going to be a White Christmas."
Above: Say "Cheese . . . and Christmas crackers."
The Lord Mayor and Lady Mayoress of 1975 set off a
chain reaction of smiles at a Christmas celebration

"Santa Claus is Coming to Town"

"He's making a list and checking it twice, Gonna find out who's naughty or nice"

Left: Ted Humpries sorts out stray presents at the GPO's 'Heartbreak Corner' in 1968, where undelivered gifts piled up
Right: Tree's company in 1976. Paul Thwaite and Jane Allwood are told they have the X (mas) Factor

Above: Margaret Beaman meets Father Christmas — Santa proudly shows off his own present to himself, a 1927 motor to deliver the prezzies by road

Right: Happy Christmas war is over in 1945. TJ's celebrate a peaceful December 24 with late night opening

To All Our Customers...
A VERY HAPPY CHRISTMAS!
..... FOR THEIR SERVICE WE ARE OPEN
TILL 5.30 p.m. TO-NIGHT, CHRISTMAS EVE

T.J. HUGHES & CO. LTD

LONDON ROAD · LIVERPOOL · 3

Above: Looking over Liverpool at Christmas, a gigantic Chris Cringle
keeps an eye on city centre shoppers in 1976

Top: An audience with Santa as a young visitor tells him that all she wants for Christmas 1963 is her two front teeth
Bottom: Excited children join mum and dad in the queue for Blackler's grotto in 1986. It will be worth the wait as they are entertained by Santa's elves along the way

"He knows when
you are sleeping,
he knows when
you're awake,
He knows if you've
been good or bad,
So be good for
goodness sake!"

Above: Plane sailing for Santa Claus as he
arrives at Liverpool Airport in 1989, mobbed
by fans from Kingsthorne Road School
Left: A store so good they named it twice –
Owen Owen remind readers in 1967 that
the countdown to Christmas is just nine days

"STAR OF WONDER, STAR OF NIGHT"

Special branch: "Blinkin' fairy lights!" It's a fir cop for this officer who helped put the finishing touches to the City's festive tree in 1953

Bright lights, big city: The spangly, spectacular illuminations provide a heavenly backdrop to Paradise Street in 1962

> *"Westward
> leading, still
> proceeding,
> Guide us to Thy
> perfect light"*

Above: The magic of a Mersey Christmas captured by award-winning photographer Stephen Shakeshaft, who had pictured the city over Yuletide for four decades
Right: Welcoming the countdown to the Twelve Days of Christmas back in 1962. But where's the maids a milking and the partridge in the pear tree?
Opposite: A towering inferno of light! A breath-taking tree dominates Church Street in 1978

Above: Dressed to thrill – one to remember at the big switch-on for Liverpool One's Christmas lights in 2008
Right: Hustle, bustle, shopping bags rustle, as shoppers make the Church Street tree a meeting point in 1975
Opposite: A luminous man in the moon shines down on shoppers in December 1969

"THERE'S NO BUSINESS LIKE SNOW BUSINESS!"

"The costumes, the scenery, the makeup, the props The audience that lifts you when you're down"

Top: Ready to ruffle feathers, Emu in Pantoland was the festive attraction at the Empire in 1975. An all-star cast featured Georgina Moon, Barbara New, Carl Wayne, Billy Dainty, and Rod Hull. Oh, and the cheeky, beaky Emu
Above: "I'm free!" John Inman cleans up at the box office – or was that the two ladies behind him? Look behind you, John. Mother Goose, 1982
Right: Mesmerised! Pure panto magic charmed the children of Bootle Community Centre in 1990 – oh yes it did!

Full of beans: Gerry Marsden left his Pacemakers behind to star with that gem of a comedian Jimmy Jewel at the Empire in 1976

Top: T-Time at the Empire in 1991. Nothing Wishee Washee about this production thanks to the star of the A-Team
Right: Ice and easy does it. Skating trio Sally Ross, Douglas Breniser and Sue Park glide across the stage in Ali Baba and the 40 Thieves, at the Empire in 1965
Opposite Top: The Rat Pack 'em in at the Empire in 1987. Roland Rat, Little and Large and two helpers push the Ratmobile to matinee performance in Dick Whittington
Opposite Bottom: Irish Diva, the lovely Dana who likes all kinds of everything, loved being Snow White with her magnificent seven dwarves at the Empire in 1988

Above: Float on – festively! The much-loved Panto Procession was a highlight
of the festive season back in 1960. Yogi Bear waves to fans in Dale Street

Above: You had to hand it to the cast of Tom Thumb – they scaled new heights in this whimsical panto at the Royal Court in 1966

CHRISTMAS DAY TELEVISION 1967

BBC 1

9.00 We Wish You A Merry Christmas: Three thousand children and the Royal Philharmonic Orchestra add up to the Robert Mayer Carol Concert.
9.30 News & Weather
9.40 Jackanory
9.55 The Sooty Show
10.15 The Charlie Chaplin Comedy Theatre
10.30 Nina and Frederik
11.00 Morning Service
From St George's Parish Church, Stockport
11.45 Leslie Crowther meets the kids in hospital at Christmas
12.30 Z Cars
12.55 News & Weather
1.05 A Spoonful of Sugar: Keith Macklin and Sheila Tracey set out to make patients dreams come true at a Richmond home for disabled ex-Servicemen.
1.35 Three Way Christmas Quiz: 'Ask the Family' winners meet 'Top of the Form' finalists
2.05 Top of the Pops: Featuring the Beatles, Engelbert Humperdinck, Petula Clark, Tom Jones, Sandie Shaw
3.00 The Queen broadcasts her Christmas message
3.10 Billy Smart's Circus
4.15 Disney Time with Dick Van Dyke
5.00 Cinderella: Jimmy Tarbuck stars as Buttons and Terry Scott and Hugh Lloyd as the Ugly Sisters
6.30 News & Weather
6.35 War On Want: James Mossman makes a Christmas appeal on behalf of the starving.
6.40 Christmas Night with the Stars
Rolf Harris introduces sketches by the casts of Till Death Us Do Part, the Illustrated Weekly Hudd, Steptoe and Son, and Beggar My Neighbour
8.40 The Ken Dodd Christmas Show
Featuring the Seekers, Graham Stark, John Laurie and Patricia Hayes, plus a bulletin from Knotty Ash
9.40 Film: The Man Who Shot Liberty Valance
11.35 News & Weather
11.40 An Astronomer's Christmas
A few reflections from Sir Bernard Lovell

"Let it Snow"

"Best place to be was at home with a warm fire, mulled wine and a mince pie or two . . . and a bone for the dog"

Left: Seacombe Ferry as winter's grip tightens in January 1982
Below: Slush hour! Snow fades to grey in 1968

Above: The ghostly outline of a masted sailing ship lurks out of the gloom on the frozen River Mersey in 1895. Only a lone family and their dog venture out to endure the bitter cold at the Egremont Landing Stage

Left: Snow go area. Two operators – one dressed for the occasion, one certainly not – brave the adverse weather to try out the new state-of-the-art automatic snow plough. True grit!

Top: "Look what we got for Christmas." Youngsters from Irby CP School return to class after the break in 1978. Maybe they would get sent home because of the bad weather — fingers crossed
Above: The majestic St George's Hall in 1977
Left: A policeman's not-so-happy lot in 1969

Above: Legendary Liverpool manager Bill Shankly and a referee
examine the Anfield pitch for the festive fixtures in 1969

Top: That Liverpudlian neighbourhood spirit
worked wonders in 1982 when the pipes
froze and everyone shared their water supply
Right: Suits you Sir, even the beard!
Tailor made for a smart Christmas,
Hepworth's had the answers in 1955

"*It's the Most Wonderful Time of the Year*"

Above: "C'mon out . . . or we'll sing another carol"
Opposite: Stunning lights provide a beautiful Christmas beacon in 1985

"There'll be parties for hosting
Marshmallows for toasting
And caroling out in the snow"

Sleigh ride: The photographer made it out with Santa just in time to capture this wonderful panoramic view in 1970

CHRISTMAS BUNLOAF

HERE is a recipe for Christmas Bunloaf the Liverpool Echo received in 1966 from Mrs Prandle of Upton – and still grateful to her for it.

Ingredients:
1lb currants (450g)
1/2lb candied peel (225g)
½ tsp bicarbonate soda
12oz plain flour (340g)
¼ tsp salt
6oz margarine and lard mixed (175g)

3oz soft brown sugar (85g)
1 tbsp each dark treacle and syrup
1 tsp mixed spice
½ tsp grated nutmeg
½ tsp cinnamon
juice and grated rind of one orange
3 eggs
A little milk

Method:
Rub the fat and flour together in a large mixing bowl and add the dry ingredients.

Stir in the fruit and peel. In a separate pan, melt the treacle and syrup with the bicarbonate of soda, add the milk and beaten eggs.

Add to the mixing bowl and stir with a large spoon to a soft consistency, adding a little milk if the mixture seems too dry.

Spoon into a large greased loaf tin and bake at Regulo 4 (180C) for about two hours, until a metal skewer inserted into the centre of the cake comes out clean. Leave the bunloaf to cool and then turn out.

Above: "When you said we were starting our own taxi service I didn't expect this." The barrow boys cope with the freezing weather on Highton Street in 1969
Right: Track suits from Jack Sharp topped the wish lists, even back in 1977. The famous Whitechapel store was in a league of its own

Above: Who's paying the lecky bill for all this? There were more than sparkling lights above Marks and Spencer in 1966 – little pixies danced in the air, or was that one shandy too many at the office party? **Left:** First to the shops to avoid that last minute panic in a picturesque Church Street, 1985

"DRIVING HOME FOR CHRISTMAS"

Above: The last Christmas of the Fifties in 1959, and the dawn of a new era

"Home is where the hearth is. Time to crack open the bubbly, tear into the selection box and hang the stockings. But first a festive game, to beat the holiday traffic . . ."

Above: Marzipan motors –
sales of de-icers went
through the roof in 1958
Right: An icicle motorcycle.
This Victoria Street rider in
1968 is not amused
Opposite Page: Twinkle
twinkle, Liverpool stars of '67

"WHAT CHRISTMAS MEANS TO ME"

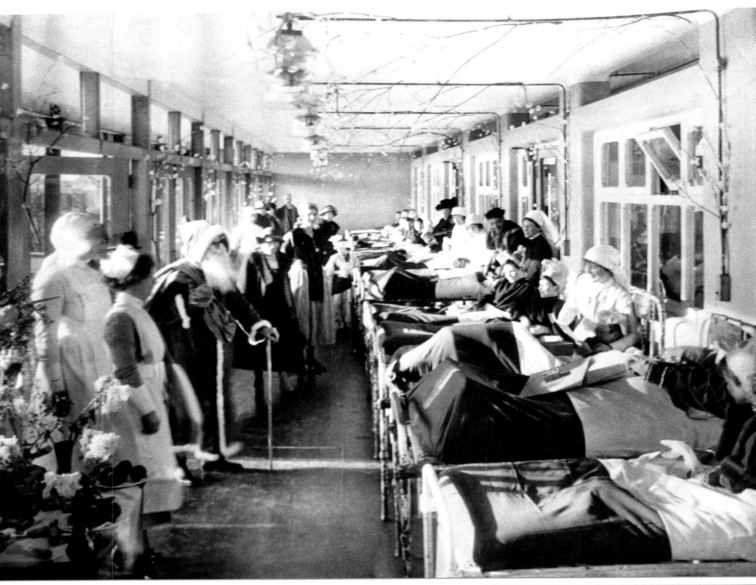

"*Wouldn't life be worth the living, Wouldn't dreams be coming true, If we kept the Christmas spirit, All the whole year through?*"

Top: A welcome visitor to Leasowe Children's Hospital in 1927 – there's no better tonic than Santa, who looks as though he should have had a check-up himself
Right: Last minute bargains from Owen Owen in 1945

Above: What the Dickens is going on – a scene from *Oliver Twist*? No, it's kind-hearted Lord Mayor Margaret Beavan handing out gifts to a poor family on Christmas Eve in 1927
Right: Sweet girls Theresa Ware and Gladys Smith of Tate & Lyle meet Father Christmas at TJ's grotto in 1958

Above: Liverpool's Lord Mayor Sydney Jones applauds the pre-war Goodfellow parcel packers in 1938
Right: The Liverpool Echo's hamper competition in 1975 brought food for thought and Connie Powell didn't mince her words when she thanked the kind sponsors – the Goodfellow Fund
Opposite page: Bags of Liverpool love – the ladies of the Goodfellow parcel depot in Jamaica Street work overtime in 1938 to spread some joy

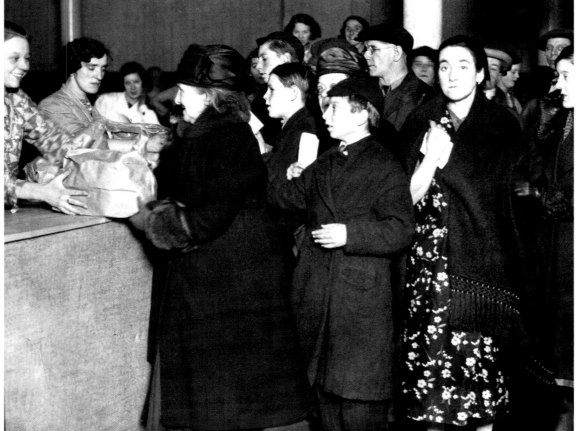

Above: Yule never celebrate alone – Bob Paisley with Graeme Souness, Bob Boulder and Phil Neal at the LFC Supporters' Club children's party, 1983. That little lad by Graeme isn't going to give up his Jammy Dodger

Left: The Goodfellows epitomised the spirit of giving at Christmas as this poignant picture from 1934 shows

Above: The long and winding road. Emergency services from the Highway Department go out to salt and grit the roads in 1963. William Brown Street is the location for the hit squad who'd rather be at home

Above: Cheers! A rum do . . . bar none, with a nautical and nice Santa tribute act. It's the Captain of the good tug Trafalgar, John French, on board the Bar Lightship Planet, toasting the crew and members of the Mersey Mission to Seamen, December 23, 1969

Above: Liverpool a lion in winter – the city that never sleeps is captured in this striking image from 1968, taken on William Brown Street

"Glories stream
from heaven afar,
Heavenly hosts
sing Alleluia!"

Above: Everyone loves the Nativity even if we all know the ending.
A happy cast at St Aidan's Preparatory School, Wallasey
Right: Hark! Two musical angels herald in the start of Christmas. Rumour
has it they are there every Christmas at Everton Heights, then disappear
on January 6
Opposite page: Christmas – with strings attached. Robert Sells conducts
the choir and orchestra at Liverpool Anglican Cathedral in 1991

Hurry! FOR THESE Value for money GIFTS

BLACKLERS

For Mum

BLANKET COATS
Big selection of styles, colourful and cosy with snug fitting hood. Amazing Value. From **£21**

COATS FOR TEENS & TWENTIES
Range of up-to-the-minute styles in the season's most popular cloths and colours. All have full skirt, tie belt and many have hoods. Sizes 10 to 16. **£17.95**

JUMPERS & OVER TOPS
By "Skylar." Long sleeved in various colours and styles. Good Value! **£5.25**

Wool Jumpers
By "Grey Deer." Turtle neck, long sleeved pure wool jumpers, various colours. Sizes 36-44". Sets. When cert. £6.95. **£4.95**

For Dad

MEN'S OVERCOATS
D.B. Shorties in plain cloths or Tweeds, also conventional style.
Shortie ... **£19.50**
Conventional **£23.75**
Larger sizes extra

"TOOTAL" SHIRTS
Super quality. Poly/Cotton shirts in a range of shades and smart patterns. **£5.95**

PULLOVERS
Crew-neck style. Shetland type — 65% wool, 35% mixed fibres. In a choice of 6 colours. **£6.50**

For Boys

BILLIARDS/SNOOKER TABLES
SAVE £20 ! 6ft. Billiards or Snooker Table, complete with legs, Snooker/Billiards Balls, Cues and Marker. USUALLY £98. **£78**

For Girls

DRESSES
Many attractive styles in assorted colours and prints. Sizes to fit ages 2 to 12 years. **£4.95 & £5.95**

For Aunt

SHORTIE NIGHTIES
Nylon Nightdresses, with a fancy nylon edging around the neckline; delightful range of colours to choose from.
W., WX., OS. **£2.40**

"Pretty Polly" 'STANDEASIES'
The tights for "gentle" support; good shades in sizes to fit 37-54 hips. Usually £1.12 **95p**
Also Stockings. Usually 95p. **80p**

Comfort Tights
"Non-stops" by "Pretty Polly" in Lycra and Tendrelle have that little extra for sheer comfort and gentle support. To fit up to 46in. hips USUALLY 77p. **69p**

Prices for all these "Pretty Polly" lines are for one day only!

For Family

WALL CLOCKS
"Westclox" Majorca battery kitchen wall clocks, with clear dial; fully guaranteed. **£6.95**

"PARKER" BALL PENS — Reduced
Famous "T" ball pens in four colours; steel cap and clip, press top action in gift case. Reduced from £1.75. **99p**

USEFUL DRAPERY GIFTS
"His" and "Hers" Terry Towels PER PAIR **£4.30**
Easy-Care Printed Table Cloths 55" x 70" EACH **£4.95**
Embroidered Pillow Cases. PER PAIR **£2.90**

STAR BUY ! ENGLISH BONE CHINA
"Royal Victoria" Fine English Bone China "Buffet Plates" in decorated patterns, all gift packed. ONLY EACH **59p**

CHRISTMAS CRACKERS
Full-Size Box of 12 decorated Crackers in assorted colours, with foil. Double contents. **59p**
Miniatures. Box of 12 Tree Crackers in assorted colours, with foils. **49p**

CHRISTMAS CARDS
BUMPER BOX. 20 assorted new season colourful cards with envelopes. **35p**
CLASSIC PACKET. 12 all large superior cards, new colourful designs, with envelopes. **32p**

PLAYPEOPLE
The fabulous Playpeople for Little People! Introductory basic set offer: e.g. Knights, Builders, etc. Usually £2.80. **£1.95**

PENCIL CASES
Very good quality, all-round zip case containing assorted pencils and school items.
Large size reduced from £1.60. **£1.15**
Medium size reduced from £1.05. **69p**

Ghosts of Christmas past: A spooky seasonal picture of Charing Cross, Birkenhead. The ghostly effect of this photo, taken in 1963, was down to time exposure . . . or was it? Left: Blackler's offered real value for money gifts – this advert from 1977 offered gifts from mum, dad, boys, girls, aunts and family. But what about uncles?

Above: Candlelight, oh candlelight – the angelic voices of the choirboys at Liverpool Cathedral's Holly Bough Service in 1964

"So let the bells ring out for Christmas!"

All the best for Christmas!

Mackintosh's always in quality street

John Mackintosh & Sons, Ltd., Toffee Town, Halifax

Above: From the North Pole to South Liverpool, the residents of Allerton were in for a treat when Santa arrived in a horse-drawn carriage in 1967 via Penny Lane
Left: Quality Street – a chocolate box full of delights back in 1945. And all the way from a wonderful Chrismassy place called Toffee Town in Halifax

73

Opposite top: Christmas cuppa and sticky bun for the children of St Alban's School, enjoying a mini-festive feast at the railway arch air shelter in the north of the city in 1941

Opposite bottom: Doddy delighted children and adults alike when he switched on the tree lights in 2008. Diddy Kevin Kirk and Lauren Wood were tickled by the master of Mirth making merry

Right: Two well wrapped up Liver Ladies make their way home through the snow in the Christmas of 1968

Below: Gifts really did grow on trees as the Liverpool Child Welfare Association hosted a party at their Copperas Hill HQ in 1955

Above: It's 1962 – the Swinging Sixties are underway and there's optimism everywhere.
Even a Santa on a lighted scaffold looks as though he is walking in the air

Above: Santa may have added specs appeal but little Bradley Morris wasn't impressed with Lewis's grotto at first. A few kind words and a prezzie and his smile soon filled the grotto in 2008

Above: Hitting the right note in aid of the Walton Hospital Leukaemia Fund were members of St John's Parish Church Choir, Egremont, at Liverpool's Philharmonic Hall in 1987

Right: Santa meets children at Lewis's grotto in 1988

Opposite Top: Poor but proud and content thanks to the kindness of strangers. The ragpickers at their Christmas dinner in 1921

Opposite Bottom: A brisk walk in the crisp morning air. A jogger and dog walkers wish each other Happy Christmas at Wavertree Playground in the snow

Merry Christmas &
Happy New Year

Great value for Christmas

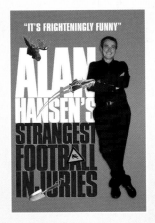